Jerome Allen

Temperament in Education

Jerome Allen

Temperament in Education

ISBN/EAN: 9783337004873

Printed in Europe, USA, Canada, Australia, Japan

Cover: Foto ©Thomas Meinert / pixelio.de

More available books at **www.hansebooks.com**

The Reading Circle Library. —

No. 11.

TEMPERAMENT IN

EDUCATION;

ALSO,

SUCCESS IN TEACHING.

BY

JEROME ALLEN, Ph.D.,

PROFESSOR OF PEDAGOGY, UNIVERSITY OF THE CITY OF NEW YORK;
ASSOCIATE EDITOR OF THE "SCHOOL JOURNAL," N. Y.

NEW YORK AND CHICAGO:

E. L. KELLOGG & CO.

1890

INTRODUCTION.

THE author lays no claim to be the originator of the facts concerning temperament. Most of these have been known for more than two thousand years. All he has tried to do is to bring together and present such admitted principles as can be used by those who wish to study children and improve themselves. The attempt is here made not to talk about temperament or talk at it, but *teach it*, as far as the printed page can be made to teach.

The simple reading of these pages will do very little good. Such use of them may serve to pass away an hour, but with little profit. The only way to make them of real educational value is to do exactly what is directed to be done. There is enough here outlined for six months' study, and at the end of that time whoever does the work will be on the way to *know himself* and those about him far better than ever before. It is a principle in psychology, that we *cannot understand in others what we do not experience first in ourselves.* The object of this paper is to give its students more intimate knowledge of themselves.

Free use in both thought and expression has been made of the following books:

"Stewart on Temperament," London, 1885.

"The Characters of Theophrastus," London, 1831.

Lavater's "Looking Glass," London, 1800; Lavater's "Essays on Physiognomy," New York, 1871.

George Bancroft's essay on "The Doctrine of Temperaments," New York, 1824.

JEROME ALLEN.

NEW YORK, Jan., 1889.

CONTENTS.

TEMPERAMENT IN EDUCATION.

THE study of temperament has occupied an important place among scholars for more than two thousand years, although it has been but recently valued on account of its educational benefits. It is now admitted to be especially useful to the teacher. Temperament takes into consideration all bodily influences as far as they show mental characteristics.

How we can Know the Mind.—We have no way of judging of the mind but by its manifestations through the body, and we can only judge what another thinks by what he does and how he looks. Individuals are frequently met whose characters are stamped upon their faces, so that by their very appearance they show what they are. Within certain limits we can judge of the thoughts of all people by outward signs. It is for the purpose of pointing out what these appearances and signs are that this treatise is written.

Great injury results from the wrong education of children. Nothing is more important than to find out as early as possible in what sphere of life a child can attain the greatest success when he arrives at maturity.

Native Characteristics of Children.—There are some boys who never could be qualified to become lawyers, but they would make excellent physicians. There are others who might attain great eminence as builders or engineers, and who would sink far below mediocrity as doctors or clergymen. The most eminent men have recognized the necessity of early deciding what a child can best do in after life. Cicero sent his son to Athens and placed him under the care of Chrysippus, who was one of the greatest philosophers of the age; but history informs us that the young man proved a blockhead, and showed that he was incapable of improving even under the instruction of so eminent a teacher.

The Proposition of Ciçero.—In view of this fact Cicero proposed "that there should be triers, or examiners, appointed by the state to inspect the genius of every bright boy and to allot him the part that is most suitable to his natural talent." It was the custom of Socrates to question his pupils for the purpose of ascertaining their thoughts and talents; and it is related that Clavius, a German mathematician, was considered a hopeless blockhead until one of his teachers tried his talents in geometry, when it was discovered in what direction his genius lay. He afterwards became one of the most eminent mathematicians of the age.

Remarks of Addison.—In 1712 Addison said in

the *Spectator* "that nothing is more usual than
to see forty or fifty boys of several ages and tem-
pers and inclinations, ranged together in the same
class, employed upon the same authors, and en-
joined the same tasks. Whatever their natural
genius may be, they are all to be made poets, his-
torians, and orators alike. They are all obliged to
have the same capacity, to bring the same couplet
or verse, and to furnish out the same portion of
prose. Every boy is bound to have as good a
memory as the captain of the form. *Instead of
adapting studies to the particular genius of the
youth, we expect from a young man that he should
adapt his genius to the studies.*" Could anything
be more applicable to our condition to-day? Addison suggests that it would be well to examine
pupils under the inspection of teachers, in reference to their capacities and temperaments, and
make such a distribution of them into proper
classes and divisions as their genius qualifies them
for, as professors, trades, engravers, or service by
land or sea. Here Addison was as wise as Cicero.

What Dr. South says.—It is remarked by Dr.
South that " some ministers run their heads against
a pulpit who might have done excellent service at
a plough-tail ; and many lawyers, failures at the
bar, might have made very elegant watermen, and
have brilliantly shined at the occupation of scrub-
bing the Temple stairs. On the other hand, he
says that he knew a corn-cutter who would have
made an excellent physician, and several tailors

that would have made good barbers, and builders rolling under their burdens who might have managed a needle with great dexterity."

The study of temperament then, is of great use to parents and teachers, and as such its outlines are here recorded. We have drawn from all sources, especially the ones mentioned in the "Introduction" to this treatise, and while we make no special acknowledgments, yet ideas and words have been taken from every place where we could get them. The arrangement is our own, many of the observations are ours; but many of the thoughts and many also of the applications we lay no claim to have originated.

HOW TO STUDY OURSELVES.

Individual Examination.—To enable us to know ourselves, each individual must make certain examinations. It would be well for each one reading this article to answer the following questions:

Am I quick or slow to perceive the point of a joke?

What is the color of my hair?

Do I know of any one whose hair is the same color as my own?

Is this person also slow or quick to perceive a joke?

What is the *texture* of my hair—fine or coarse?

Notice now whether there is any relation between the fineness or coarseness of the hair and quickness of perception.

In fully determining this question and its implied relations, you must examine several persons, and make the following observations carefully and deliberately:

A Sanguine Temperament.—First find a person whose complexion is florid, whose skin is fair, with blue eyes, light hair, animated countenance, bright-red lips, and active and easily excited circulation; a person who blushes readily, whose muscular fibres are firm without rigidity and elastic without feebleness.   If possible, find one who fills all of these conditions: it may not be easy at first to do this, but by a little searching such a one will be discovered among your acquaintances.   This individual should have a well-developed figure, and a head and nose a little larger than usual, broad chin and cheeks, ruddy complexion, and inclined to grow fleshy as he grows older.   The hair of such a person will be soft, and not much, if at all, curly, of a pale color, and often passing through different shades to red.   The skin will be smooth and often white, the eyes usually blue, and the habit of the body soft and plump.   The strength of the whole body will be moderate, and exercise will readily bring perspiration.   All of these peculiarities can be found after a little searching, and it will be necessary to *study* such an individual ; making observations in writing, if you desire to make thorough work, and ascertain the following points :

Questions.—Is this person irritable, or cheerful, or morose ; unsteady in purpose, or steady and persistent?   Is he full of spirits, outspoken, frank and joyous, with "a kind of impetuosity of temper," or is he the opposite?

Would you judge that the one you have selected is a steady, calm, quiet person, not much elevated in emotion, and not often very much depressed ; never laughing immoderately, and never crying ; or the opposite?

Would such an individual as this make a good lawyer or a judge, or a good teacher; or, on the other hand, would he be more likely to make a good mechanic, a good bridge-builder, a good engineer, or a faithful day-laborer?

By examining carefully the characteristics of such an individual as this, you will come to the following general conclusions, viz.:

Conclusions.—The strength of the whole body is but moderate; the mind is sensible, although often irritable, yet cheerful, and unsteady. The spirits are full, but liable to sudden changes; frank and joyous, sometimes becoming quite angry. We shall have more to say about this temperament farther on.

The Bilious Temperament.—Having finished for a time your examination of the sanguine temperament, turn your attention to another, and find some person who has black curling hair, dark eyes, a swarthy and at the same time ruddy complexion, and thick rough hair and skin, and a strong, full pulse. The eyes of such an individual should be black or dark brown, the complexion may be dark or darkish, and the face may be often pale olive, and perhaps square. The nose may be outspread, the neck short, and the whole build thick-set. The peculiarities of the face and nose and neck and build are usually nearly the same in all the temperaments, so that these peculiarities must not be relied upon in order to determine the temperament as much as the color of the hair and the eyes and complexion. Having found such a person as this, ascertain the following facts:

Questions.—Is he impulsive or the opposite? Is he seriously inclined—thoughtful? or, on the other hand, is he given to thoughts of levity without much reason or thoughtfulness? Does he jump at conclusions and then change them as soon as he arrives at them, or are his conclusions thoughtfully arrived at?

In business matters is he cool and wary, or is he chimerical, hasty, frequently making serious blunders, rushing on "where angels fear to tread"? Is he passionate or dispassionate? Jealous, revengeful, and unscrupulous, or the opposite? Is he eager, earnest, and persistent? or careless and intermittent?

Does he endure in his work from day to day and even from year to year? or does he frequently change and become discouraged in his pursuits? Does he prefer business or profitable occupations, or intellectual pursuits, or otherwise?

Is he happy or miserable? In the pursuit or attainment of wealth, power, and family welfare is he decided or undecided in speech, always ready and well informed on the subject with which he is most conversant, or is he undecided and never ready, and always liable to make mistakes?

Lymphatic Temperament.—Now let the bilious temperament rest for a while, and find a person who has light, sandy, or white hair, light-gray eyes, having a pallid and perhaps an unhealthy whiteness of skin, which is almost bereft of hair, and small blood vessels; having a weak, slow pulse, cold surfaces, general defect of vital functions. Such a person may have flaccid muscles, more or less pallor of countenance; he will probably be slow-moving and pale-faced, his hair may sometimes be fair brown, but is always thin, and his eyes a brown-gray, or light hazel, thinly colored, the white often in too great proportion, and lustreless.

Questions.—Now ascertain the following points : Is his memory good or poor? What about his reasoning powers? Is his judgment sound and logical? Has he a character for common-sense and straightforward, direct dealings with his fellowmen? Socially does he make the best of company, and yet is he a good friend? Is he impulsive or slow and heavy; are his conclusions thoughtfully arrived at or the opposite? Is he excitable, readily provoked? On the other hand, is he not excitable and not easily provoked; readily forgiving, but never forgetting? Is he persistent, although not ardent? How about his business habits? Does he endure keeping at his work day by day, or is hard labor rather avoided? Do personal comforts and indulgences make him happy, or is he careless about it? Is he slow of speech and always well informed, or does he speak very quickly and very rapidly, and seldom certain about what he says?

Nervous Temperament.—Now select another person having fine susceptibilities, great rapidity of

action, ideas, and of speech; in the expression of
his feelings and ideas having great vividness of
imagination. Such a person will have small muscles, but great vivacity of sensation, sudden and
changeable determinations and judgments. Find
one whose face tapers from a high or broad forehead down to a thin chin; small features, long
neck and slight figure. The hair should be light
brown, the eyes gray, and the complexion pale,
and clear; the body must not be at all inclined to
corpulency, but should rather be tall and extremely
thin.

Questions.—Now having found such a person
determine the following conditions: Is this individual impulsive, animated, rapid, or the opposite?
Are conclusions drawn so hastily that they are
often regretted, or does he draw his conclusions
slowly and never regrets a step he has taken? Is
he soon excited and readily provoked, or the opposite? If he becomes excited is he soon reconciled,
or does he hold a grudge for years? Is he imaginative, sensitive, particularly fastidious, or the
opposite? Is he resolute or irresolute? Is he
persistent after a final decision, enduring in work,
never giving up, and in danger of physical bank-
ruptcy, or the opposite? Are intellectual and
muscular pursuits enjoyed more or less than eat-
ing or drinking. 2. From what source does this individual get his happiness, from what enriches the
mind, or what enriches the pocket; from travel,
art, or literature, or from the delights of a good

table? Is his speech rapid—often very rapid, or slow—frequently very slow? Is he undecided or decided; and does precision often give place to fancy?

THE SANGUINE TEMPERAMENT.

Physical Characteristics.	Mental Characteristics.
1. Hair. Red, or red- ish. 2. Color. Eyes. Blue. 3. Complexion. More or less florid. (Color of the face.) 4. Face. Square, 5. Form. Nose. Outspread. 6. Neck. Short. 7. * Build. Thick-set.	1. Impulsive. Buoyant and cheerful. Favorable conclusions thoughtlessly drawn. 2. Excitable. Readily provoked. Easily reconciled. Emotional. 3. Ardent in everything. Not persistent. 4. Not enduring in work. 5. Muscular pursuits preferred to intellectual. 6. Equally happy in the pursuit of little as of great ends. More happy in pursuit than enjoyment. 7. F i r m, outspoken speech. Not minutely informed.

* The same in the Sanguine, the Bilious, and the Lym phatic.

THE BILIOUS TEMPERAMENT.

(The Cʜᴏʟᴇʀɪᴄ, from Cʜᴏʟᴇʀ-Bɪʟᴇ.)

Physical Characteristics.	Mental Characteristics.
1. **Hair.** Black. 2. **Eyes.** Black or dark brown. 3. *Color.* **Complexion.** Dark or darkish. (Color of the face.) "Pale olive." —*Laycock*.	1. Not impulsive. Serious. Conclusions thoughtfully a r-rived at. 2. "Passionate, jealous, revengeful, unscrupulous." In business matters, cool and wary.
4. **Face.** Square. 5. *Form.* **Nose.** Outspread. 6. **Neck.** Short. 7. * **Build.** Thick-set.	3. Eager, earnest, persistent. 4. Enduring in work. 5. Business or gainful pursuits preferred to muscular or intellectual, but able to excel in all. 6. Happy in the pursuit and attainment of wealth, power, and family welfare. 7. Decided speech. Always ready, and informed.

* The same in the Sanguine, the Bilious, and the Lymphatic.

THE LYMPHATIC TEMPERAMENT.

(PHLEGMATIC.)

Physical Characteristics.	Mental Characteristics.
1. 〔 *Hair.* Fair brown (flaxen).	1. Not impulsive. Slow. Heavy. Conclusions thoughtfully arrived at.
2. *Eyes.* Brown gray (green or light hazel). Thinly colored. The white often in too great proportion. Lustreless. "Dim-eyed."	2. Not excitable. Not readily provoked. Forgives, but never forgets.
	3. Persistent, not ardent.
	4. Enduring in work. A plodder in business.
3. *Complexion.* Colorless; dense. (Color of the face.) Opaque.	5. Muscular pursuits avoided.
	6. Happy from personal comforts and indulgence.
4. 〔 *Face.* Square.	7. Slow manner of speech. Always informed.
5. *Nose.* Outspread.	
6. *Neck.* Short.	
7. * *Build.* Thick-set.	

(Color. | Form.)

* The same in the Sanguine, the Bilious, and the Lymphatic.

THE NERVOUS TEMPERAMENT.

Physical Characteristics.	Mental Characteristics.
1. _Hair_ Light brown. 2. _Eyes._ Gray. (Color) 3. _Complexion._ Pale. Clear. (Color of the face.)	1. Impulsive. Animated. Rapid. Conclusion, so hastily drawn that they are often regretted. 2. Excitable. Readily provoked. Reconciled immediately. Imaginative. Sensitive. Particular. Fastidious. 3. Irresolute. Persistent after final decision. 4. Enduring in work; will never give in. In danger of physical bankruptcy. 5. Intellectual and muscular pursuits. 6. Happiness from whatever pleases the senses and enriches the mind—Travel, Art, Literature. 7. Speech rapid, often very rapid. Frequently undecided. Precision gives place to fancy.
4. _Face._ Tapers to a narrow chin from a high or broad forehead.* 5. _Nose._ Narrow. (Form) 6. _Neck._ Long. 7. _Build._ Slight. Slim. Never corpulent. Often tall and extremely thin.	

* The forehead being large compared with the rest of the face, the Nervous is sometimes called the Cerebral Temperament.

SANGUINE AND BILIOUS TEMPERAMENT.

Hair, ... Red or reddish.
Complexion, . . More or less florid.
Face, ... Square.
Nose, ... Outspread.
Neck, ... Short.
Build, ... Heavy (thick-sct).
(Six Sanguine characteristics: *see scheme.*)
Eyes, ... Black or dark brown.
(One Bilious characteristic: *see scheme.*)

SANGUINE AND NERVOUS TEMPERAMENT

Hair, ... Red or reddish.
Eyes, ... Blue.
Complexion, . . . More or less florid.
Nose, ... Outspread.
(Four Sanguine characteristics: *see scheme.*)
Face, ... Tapering from a high or broad
forehead to a narrow chin.
Neck, ... Long.
Build, ... Slim.
(Three Nervous characteristics, *see previous table.*)

SANGUINE, BILIOUS, AND NERVOUS TEMPERA-MENT.

Hair, ... Red or reddish.
Complexion, . . More or less florid.
Face, ... Square.
Neck, ... Short.
Build, ... Heavy (thick-set).

(Five Sanguine characteristics: *see scheme.*)

Eyes, ...   Black.

(One Bilious characteristic.)

Nose, ...   Narrow.

(One Nervous characteristic.)

COMPOUND COLOR CHARACTERISTICS.

(THE HAIR.)

1. Dark red, . .   Sanguine and Bilious charac-
   (red and black.)   teristics.
2. Fair red, . .   Sanguine and Lymphatic char-
   (red and sandy.)   acteristics.
3. Brown, . . .   Sanguine and Nervous charac-
   (red and gray.)   teristics.
4. Dark brown, .   Bilious and Lymphatic char-
   (black and sandy.)   teristics.

(THE EYES.)

1. Dark blue, . .   Sanguine and Bilious charac-
   (blue and black.)   teristics.
2. Brown, . . .   Bilious and Lymphatic char-
   (black and brown gray.)   [acteristics.
3. Dark gray, . .   Bilious and Nervous charac-
   (black and gray.)   teristics.

A BALANCED TEMPERAMENT.—I.

Face.   Oval.   The blended square
                            and tapering faces
                            of the four tempera-
                            ments.

Build.   Medium.   The blended stout and
                            slim builds of the
                            four temperaments,

Nose.	Outspread.	Sanguine, Bilious, and Lymphatic.
Neck.	Long.	Nervous.
Hair.	Black.	Bilious.
Eyes.	Blue.	Sanguine.
Complexion.	Colorless.	Lymphatic.

A BALANCED TEMPERAMENT.—II.

Face.	Oval.	The blended square and tapering faces of the four temperaments.
Build.	Medium.	The blended stout and slim builds of the four temperaments.
Nose.	Outspread.	Sanguine, Bilious, and Lymphatic.
Neck.	Long.	Nervous.
Hair.	Fair brown. (flaxen)	Lymphatic.
Eyes.	Blue.	Sanguine.
Complexion.	Dark.	Bilious.

A BALANCED TEMPERAMENT.—III.

Face.	Oval.	The blended square and tapering faces of the four temperaments.
Build.	Medium.	The blended stout and slim builds of the four temperaments.
Nose.	Narrow.	Nervous.

Neck.	Long.	Nervous.
Hair.	Dark red.	Sanguine and Bilious.
Eyes.	Dark blue.	Sanguine and Bilious.
Complexion.	Colorless.	Lymphatic.

THE SEMI-BALANCED SANGUINE TEMPERA-MENT.

Face.	Oval.	The blended square and tapering faces of the four temperaments.
Build.	Medium.	The blended stout and slim builds of the four temperaments.
Hair.	Reddish.	Sanguine.
Eyes.	Blue.	Sanguine.
Complexion.	Florid.	Sanguine.
Nose.	Narrow	Nervous.
Neck.	Long.	Nervous.

THE SEMI-BALANCED BILIOUS TEMPERAMENT.

Face.	Oval.	The blended square and tapering faces of the four temperaments.
Build.	Medium.	The blended stout and slim builds of the four temperaments.
Hair.	Black.	Bilious.
Eyes.	Black.	Bilious.
Complexion.	Dark.	Bilious.
Nose.	Narrow.	Nervous.
Neck.	Long.	Nervous.

THE SEMI-BALANCED LYMPHATIC TEMPERA-MENT.

Face.	Oval.	The blended square and tapering faces of the four temperaments. .
Build.	Medium.	The blended stout and slim builds of the four temperaments.
Hair.	Sandy.	Lymphatic.
Eyes.	Light hazel.	Lymphatic.
Complexion.	Colorless.	Lymphatic.
Nose.	Narrow.	Nervous.
Neck.	Long.	Nervous.

THE SEMI-BALANCED NERVOUS TEMPERA-MENT.

Face.	Oval.	The blended square and tapering faces of the four temperaments.
Build.	Medium.	The blended stout and slim builds of the four temperaments.
Hair.	Light brown.	Nervous.
Eyes.	Gray.	Nervous.
Complexion.	Pale and clear.	Nervous.
Nose.	Narrow.	Nervous.
Neck.	Long.	Nervous.

THE BEST TEMPERAMENT.

It may be asked, Which is the best temperament? The reply is not doubtful. The compound in equal proportions of the four pure temperaments—*the balanced temperament*—is certainly the best for its possessor, for in it the four temper each another, and the troublesome special tendencies or impulses that characterize every pure temperament are toned down to comfortable smoothness of action.

The impulsiveness of the Sanguine is tempered by the inaction of the Lymphatic; the eye-to-business, position, and power of the Bilious, by the imagination of the Nervous; the love of ease and contentment with personal comforts of the Lymphatic, by the ambition of the bilious; the perplexity and indecision of the Nervous from seeing too many ways open, by the impulsiveness of the Sanguine.

That surely is the best temperament whose action avoids extremes; has sufficient of the natural force of all the pure temperaments to acquire any kind of knowledge; is well fitted for any profession or business; retains through life the natural figure, and has equal health, free from the tendency or predisposition that every pure temperament has to disease or derangement of its special organ.

Such is the BALANCED TEMPERAMENT.

SELF-STUDY.

Having pursued the study of temperament up to this point, by observing others, it will now be necessary for the student to turn his attention to himself. Prepare an outline like this :

(Name here.)   **TEMPERAMENT.**

Physical Characteristics.	Mental Characteristics.
1. *Hair.*	1.
2. *Eyes.*	2. 3.
3. *Complexion.*	4. 5.
4. *Face.*	6.
5. *Nose.*	7. 8.
6. *Neck.*	9. 10.
7. *Build.*	*etc.*

As the space under Mental Characteristics will not be sufficient to write all the answers necessary, fill up the paper with the answers to the following questions, and if you are not perfectly satisfied concerning yourself in reference to any one point, consult some intimate friend. This thorough self-study will give you more knowledge of your mental, spiritual, and physical make-up than anything else possibly could. It should be for your own eyes—none others. The answers may be destroyed after they have been written and read; but the benefit derived from such a study as this will depend on the degree of honest and faithful effort made to answer them. They may seem too minute, but after considerable experience in studying and teaching temperament the author is of the opinion their number should be extended rather than diminished.

Personal Questions. — 1. Are you impulsive? This means not only are you quick in bodily movements, but do you make up your mind without much meditation and apparently without much reason; and do you act when under a sudden impulse without thinking, sometimes doing things on the "spur of the moment"?

2. Are you more ready to draw favorable conclusions than unfavorable ones, or are you looking out for faults in others more than for good qualities?

3. Do you notice readily any peculiarity about another person, such as walk, look, speech, or dress; and are you accustomed to talk about these peculiarities to others, or do they pass from your mind without much attention?

4. Are you buoyant and cheerful, looking out for the laughable side of things, always making other people happy, sometimes inclined to be frivolous and light, or is your character the opposite?

5. Are you easily provoked, do small things

rouse your anger, and then after you have expended your wrath are you easily reconciled ? In other words, are you excitable ?

6. Are you emotional, a little inclined to be sentimental, that is, do you like to read poetry containing sentimental protestations of love and affection ; or are you rather inclined to the opposite feeling ? In selecting your reading do you take those works that are sober, sedate, descriptive, and thoughtful ; or do you rather like to read those that are of an opposite nature, such as famous murder cases and sensational love-stories ?

7. Are you ardent in everything, or only in some things; that is, do you pursue with great earnestness certain subjects and certain pursuits, and feel a great indifference to certain other subjects and other pursuits ? If this is your character, state on paper what those pursuits are that you love most. There are certain poems you love far beyond all others : write the names of three or four. There are certain other poems and books that you do not like—that you really "cannot bear to read:" what are these ?

8. Are you enduring in work ? This means whether an enterprise that you undertook last year is not completed to-day and has almost passed from your mind, or do you feel that when any work is undertaken you *must* keep at it until it is properly finished ? Have you a dozen things lying around half done which you "intend to do as soon as you find time," or is your work pretty well finished as

far as you have gone in life ? Do you frequently commence a book and after reading a few pages throw it down with the exclamation, "I don't like that book and don't intend to read it"? It is very important for you to decide your peculiarities in this particular.

9. Are muscular pursuits preferred to intellectual? Do you like to make a box, or build a house, or cultivate land, more than to write letters and study science and art ? Are your muscles firm, well developed, strong? Are you able to lift heavy weights without much difficulty, or are your muscles flaccid and weak, and do you feel disinclined to muscular exercise ? Do you like to lie abed in the morning late, feeling a reluctance to rise and commence the duties of the day, or do you open your eyes in the morning with the feeling "I am glad it is daylight so that I can commence my work, which I want so much to complete to-day"?

10. Do you like bathing, especially bathing in cold water ; or do you prefer a warm bath, in the warm part of the day, in a warm room ?

11. Are you equally happy in the pursuit of small as well as of great things—in other words, do you take as much delight in making a tidy or in fashioning a toy or in making a box as in organizing a benevolence or conducting a Sabbath-school, or arranging the classes in a public school, or in starting a reading club which will lead many boys and girls to get a love for good literature ? Do small home affairs make you

more happy than large church and society affairs? Do you enjoy home more than society, or do you rather like to be in a large company, talking and having a good time, more than being at home by yourself working at some useful occupation?

12. When you have accomplished a work do you find more happiness in its results than you had in its pursuit; in other words, does an accomplished end make you happier than the work of accomplishing that end? This is a very important question, and one that must be decided after careful thought. Do not be in haste, but consult yourself, and perhaps talk with some confidential friend.

13. Do you express your words firmly, decidedly, and outspokenly, saying sometimes with a loud voice what you think is right and what you think is wrong; and in taking this course do you feel at times disregardful of the opinions of others, particularly desirous that your own opinions should be known and respected, without much regard as to whether the opinions of other people are known or respected or not?

14. Are you minutely and carefully informed, or do you draw your conclusions without sufficient evidence, oftentimes taking supposition in place of argument? Do you conclude that a certain thing must be so, as though it was so, when afterward you find out that your conclusions were wrong and your actions were many times out of place? This is a very important point to be decided in reference to your mental make-up.

15. Are you of a jealous disposition, passionate ?
This may be determined by asking whether you
feel very deeply when a person occupies a place
that you imagine you ought to occupy, or when
some one is placed before you who, you think,
does not deserve advancement as much as yourself. It is difficult sometimes to answer these delicate questions, but if you desire to improve you
must be willing to know the truth concerning
yourself, even though that truth sometimes hurts
your pride.

16. How are you in reference to business matters ? Are you cool, wary, persistent, or are you
hasty, careless ? Do you keep an account of the
money you receive and the money you spend, and
once in a while balance accounts and see where
you could curtail your outgoes and increase your
incomes ?

17. Are you in general eager, earnest, and persistent ? This does not mean are you ardent, so
much as are you in dead earnest when you undertake a thing ? There are some people who are
very ardent, but they are not earnest; there needs
to be a careful discrimination, here and in examining yourself you should ascertain the truth in this
particular.

18. Do you like gainful pursuits—those that
bring in the money ; and are you looking out for
means to make money ; and do you value pecuniary
rewards more than praise, or the rewards of an ap-
proving conscience ? And also, do you like gainful

pursuits that do not require muscular but rather intellectual excellence? In other words, would you prefer to write for papers or write books, rather than to engage in carpentry or farming or sewing or keeping house?

19. Are you ready to forgive, but do you say I can never forget?

20. Do personal comforts and good living, pleasant rooms and agreeable surroundings, satisfy you, make you happy? Of course every one more or less values these comforts, but do you think that this feature of your character is excessive?

21. Are you usually informed in reference to every-day matters? Are you ready to answer questions that every one ought to know—as the distance to certain places, or the price of certain articles, or the standing of certain authors, or the method of working certain examples in arithmetic; or do you frequently find yourself unable to answer these questions at once, obliged to wait awhile, and collect your thoughts—perhaps investigate?

22. Do you take more pleasure from what pleases the senses—as the eye, the ear, taste, or hand—than you do from that which engages the mind? In other words, would you rather see a good play or spectacular performance where there is good music and good speaking, than to read a good author alone or with a friend?

Now, and last, select and copy from the following words those that more nearly apply to you. Add others from the questions just asked. This will help you in deciding more accurately your mental characteristics.

Impulsive. Animated. Excitable. Rapid in walk and in speech. Particular. Sensitive. Fastidious. Irresolute. Enduring. Happiness from travelling, from art, from literature, from intellectual pursuits, from muscular pursuits. A plodder in business. Slow of speech. Passionate. Etc., etc.

HOW TO IMPROVE.

Space will only permit us to give a very few suggestions under this head, although much more could be said with profit than room can be found to say.

1. If you are impulsive, and accustomed to make up your mind without much meditation, you should be careful about your bodily conditions : keep the system in perfect order, sleep more and, get more control over the will as far as possible ; think, "I must speak more slowly, I must walk more slowly." Associate with persons of slow speech, and notice their excellences. Vigilance will be the price of success.

2. If you are liable to draw unfavorable conclusions more readily than favorable ones, you must accustom yourself to look on the good side of people rather than on the bad side. You will find no one who has not in him something good; if you are tempted to say something unfavorable about any one, stop and think, and instead of saying it, *say something good.* Keep at this, and you will change in the course of a year your habit of thinking in this particular.

3. If you have an unpleasant habit of noticing little things about persons that are unnecessary to notice, you can correct this by avoiding to talk on

this subject at all. If you do not say a word, you will find your thoughts very soon changing to another channel; but it is well also to be particular in reference to what you *think about.* This habit will be of great use to you in your work in life.

4. If you are frivolous and light, you can easily check this by avoiding the companionship of those who waste their time in unprofitable conversation; a great deal of our character depends upon those with whom we associate. Frivolous people who associate with frivolous people intensify their characters. Read sober books *that interest you:* by no means force yourself to read those books that are uninteresting. The character of your reading will help you in this particular very much.

5. If you are easily provoked and small things rouse you to anger, you can correct this by a process of reasoning. After you have had a fit of anger over something that is really of no consequence, sit down and think "what a fool I made of myself! I had no reason to get angry, or at least very little occasion for it, and it would have been far better if I had kept still. The thing I was angry about would have righted itself in a very short time if left alone." In other words, bring yourself before the bar of your own judgment and condemn your conduct in the strongest terms, and do so every time you fall into fits of unreasonable anger. If you keep up this faithfully for a year, you will change your whole manner of thinking and acting in this particular.

6. If you are sentimental, you must not read sentimental poetry or stories, or associate with sentimental persons. Stop it at once, for there is nothing worse for a person than to be carried away by mere sentiment. But, on the other hand, if you are too cold and distant, wanting in love and emotion, it is your duty to read something sentimental, even though it be at first distasteful to you. Read it over and over again, until you come to absorb what is good in the sentiment and value it for its own sake. A cold and distant person will never make friends, neither will a very sentimental person. The golden mean is the true way.

7. If you pursue some things with great earnestness, and neglect other things, you can correct the habit by an effort of the reason and will: make up your mind that the thing that you neglected to-day must be done,—that is, if it is of importance to be done,—and go about it; *drop everything possible until it is done,* and then never commence anything unless you are determined to finish it. If you are not enduring in work you will not succeed. You must determine by a strong effort of the will to do what your judgment tells you you ought to do, and do it in spite of a strong inclination you may have to omit the doing of it.

8. If you do not like bathing, but rather are inclined to effeminacy, you can overcome this by gymnastic exercises, out-of-door sports, and a following of the laws of hygiene and health. Reason about your health, and say, " It is for my advan-

tage that I should become more muscular or more able to stand cold;" and then follow persistently the laws of health and the advice, if necessary, of a physician—but usually the ordinary laws of health are known so well that it is not necessary to pay for medical advice unless you are sick. The reason so many people fail in health is because a great many are not willing to live up to the light they have. They follow ease and inclination rather than duty and principle.

9. If you are timid, and feel that your opinions are of no account, and always inclined to shrink from public gaze, and never express your thoughts even though you are conscious you have better ones than you hear others express, you can overcome this by appealing to your sense of duty. It is your duty to say at the proper time, decidedly, what you know to be the right. You need not be obtrusive—you should not be ; but there are plenty of opportunities for you to express your thoughts, and express them decidedly, *and in a firm tone of voice.* This will help you. Your thinking and indecision of speech come from a want of clearness of apprehension. If you make up your mind that a certain thing is right, *and say so,* you will be led more clearly to see what is right than you could be as long as you are accustomed to be half decided and unwilling to express your opinions. None will think any less of you for a positive expression of what you believe to be the truth. In fact, no one thing will add more to your success in

life than the speaking of the truth decidedly and earnestly on all proper occasions, and yet in love.

10. If you are not minutely informed, you can easily become so by mental decision. Commence with one or two things, and inform yourself about them until *you* KNOW *what you know.* Never under any circumstances express an opinion until you are positive you know that what you say is exactly the truth. This will cure you of the defect of frequently saying that a thing is so when afterward you find out to your chagrin that it is not at all what you said it was. *Do not be afraid to say* " I DO NOT KNOW."

GENERAL SUGGESTIONS.

Self-improvement is accomplished by—

1. Knowing in what respects we ought to improve. As this treatise considers somewhat bodily functions as well as mental conditions, we shall confine ourselves here to physical conditions. Find out in what respects your bodily actions hinder the normal workings of the mind and heart. It may be that you should consult a physician, for our mental states are much dependent on our bodily organizations and conditions. Having ascertained, both by your own introspection and knowledge, and the aid you can get from others, in what respects you ought to improve, then set yourself about the work of improvement *with a will.* Commence with one thing at a time. Many fail because they attempt too much at once. If you are very hasty in speech, commence with this, and use the means to correct the defect; or if you are accustomed to draw hasty conclusions, go at this; or if your memory fails you, then take the means to correct this. Don't try too many things at a time, or you will fail in all. A thorough course of mental, spiritual, and bodily training, in order to accomplish the greatest good, *must take time.*

2. Be careful in reference to your associates. If you are slow and logy, and cannot command your thoughts readily, and draw your conclusions with great difficulty, then associate with persons of opposite characteristics, and not with those of like qualities as yourself. Much injury is done to nervous people by associating with nervous people, and to phlegmatic temperaments by associating with other phlegmatic temperaments. The golden mean is what we should seek in self-improvement. The ideal human being has never yet appeared, except as we find it in the person of Christ, whose character as a man is so high that it is difficult for us to attain anywhere near it. The lives of great men show us that even the wisest have had many idiosyncrasies. At best we can only attain an imperfect perfection.

3. Carefully choose your reading : much depends upon this. We become very much like our ideals, and our ideals are mainly formed through the books we read. As a rule, we should only read what we like to read. It may seem impossible to like what we dislike. A little thought will show that what we dislike is not what we imagined it is.

We often dislike a certain kind of reading because we are ignorant of what it is. We frequently imagine we dislike certain persons, simply because we do not know what these persons are like. An inveterate novel-reader will devour one class of novels, and never think that his taste could be changed. The same may be said of those who are in love with mathematical, historical, or philosophical pursuits. There is a great deal in the temper of reading. By this we mean that there should be an equalization in what we read. We should like what is useful to us, and always remember that what is useful will be interesting if we properly go at it.

4. Self-improvement depends upon the will: persons of weak will can never be different from what they are. They will go along year after year, intensifying peculiarities. With a knowledge of defects there must be a strong will to remedy these defects, if improvement is expected. A vigorous will is an evidence of intelligence, but it should be remembered that *will power is not wilfulness.* The exercising of will power is an exercise of the whole mind, but the exercise of wilfulness is action with little or no mind in it. An animal very low down in the scale of intelligence may show great wilfulness, and so may an idiot; and wherever we find wilfulness either in mature or immature persons, it is an evidence of very imperfect mental action. An intelligent will properly intensified will be a force that will remedy a thousand defects. This is a most important suggestion.

5. Incidentally it should be remarked that cleanliness, correct dressing, and proper appearance are essential to the highest mental and spiritual success. It is one of the elements of self-knowledge

to know how to dress properly. Thousands of teachers have failed to make the best impression upon their pupils and the best improvement, because they have not known how to present themselves properly before their pupils. A very homely person well dressed will appear to be quite good-looking, whereas a good-looking and even quite handsome person may carry the impression of being homely on account of some incongruity of dress, appearance, or speech.

HOW TO STUDY CHILDREN.

Its Importance.—In directing the growth of children we learn much from plant-life. There must be good soil, careful nurture at first, good seed, proper amount of sunshine, rain, and shade. Not all should be treated alike. How unnatural it would be to treat young tomatoes, onions, peas, beans, corn, and trees in the same manner. It is true there is not as much difference between children as between the various forms of plant-life; but there are great differences—so great, we can see, that no two children can safely have the same treatment. Here is a girl with black eyes, dark hair, stout and robust, full of laughter, fun, and frolic; by her side is another of the same age, but with very light complexion, white or red hair, slim, demure, and often sad. It cannot for a moment be supposed that these two children will thrive under the same treatment : what will be food to one will be poison to the other.

There are four classes of boys and girls, as there are four classes of mature men and women : THE NERVOUS, THE SANGUINE, THE LYMPHATIC, AND THE BILIOUS.

It is first of all necessary to determine what the temperament of the child is, and then to give the child such treatment as will promote its healthy growth.

In What Particular Children are Alike.

All healthy children are hungry.

They are generally trustful. If found distrustful, it may be certain there is something wrong in their development.

As a rule, they are kind to animals and fond of them. Native, inborn cruelty is rare.

Children like other children better than older people.

They are very imaginative.

Get a great amount of pleasure from little things.

Naturally not afraid, at first, except of falling. It is strange that all infants before they have had any experience of life seem to possess the instinctive fear of falling. There have been various theories accounting for the cause of this, but none, as far as we know, have satisfactorily explained the fact.

Love all kinds of muscular motions.

Have little patience.

Restless under restraint.

Affectionate, often loving very uncouth and unattractive things.

In all children, taste is the first sense that is fully developed, and sight is the last. Greediness is in consequence of the early development of the sense of taste.

The auditory sensations are, next to taste, the earliest developed.

Much time is needed for children to learn to see things correctly.

Delight in rhythmical, not necessarily musical, sounds.

All children delight in a sense of ownership.

A FEW FACTS IN CHILD-GROWTH.

CUTANEOUS SENSIBILITY CAUSING A SENSE OF PAIN.

Instinctive Senses:
I. { Desire for sleep. / Desire for food. / Inborn fear of falling. }
II. { Seeing. / Hearing. / Tasting. / Smelling. }

Whether there is seeing, hearing, tasting, and smelling at first is a question; but it is at least certain that these senses are quite dull and slow in action in the very young child.

Sentiments: {
Anger.
Jealousy.
Sympathy, first manifested towards animals—a doll, often, more than for a fallen horse. It is not a moral emotion when first exhibited.
Love.
Wilfulness.
}

Anger often shows itself when the child is quite young.

Jealousy does not usually manifest itself until the child is about a year old.

Pure affection is of slow growth. When first

exhibited it has little disinterestedness in it; but when it commences to grow it matures quite rapidly. Affection is much stronger in children towards human beings than towards inferior animals, as cats and dogs.

Native Intellectual Endowments:
- Curiosity, inquisitiveness.
- Desire, selfishness.
- Talkativeness.
- Capacity for self-entertainment.
- Recognition of its dual self.
- Led by motives more or less strong.

Early Acquired Intellectual Endowments:
- Perception. } Memory, (of the actual).
- Comparison. }
- Rudimentary reasoning, both synthetic and analytic.
- Reflective powers, both synthetic and analytic, leading to generalization, (rudimentary).
- Little ideality, and so, little imagination for the first three or four years.

Later Acquired Endowments:
- Power of discriminating between the different feelings and emotions.
- Power of knowing things, and what they suggest.
- Power of knowing the true from the false, the real from the unreal and deceptive, (moral perception).
- The power of determining intelligently as to what is best or not best, (moral and intellectual will-power.)

A few facts.—1. Perception can only be strengthened by constant exercise. In some persons it remains in an immature condition all the life.

2. The memory is strong as soon as *perception, association,* and *comparison* are developed. Let a child see a thing or a fact *distinctly,* associate it with something else it has seen distinctly, or in other words, something which it *knows;* and then let him compare the two, and *he will remember.* Let our readers try this experiment and determine the truth of this statement. Poor memories in children, as well as mature people, are *results.* Remove the causes.

3. The order of mental growth is (*a*) the power of feeling, (*b*) the power of knowing, and (*c*) the power of determining. It must be always remembered that spasmodic cases of wilfulness in children give no indication as to the power of determining. This comes much later in life.

4. Effective reasoning powers are not developed until the reflective powers are somewhat mature. What does this mean? Just this, viz., that before a child can undertake to solve the problems in arithmetic that require much effort, he must be able to perceive things correctly and clearly, be able to recall his perceptions with ease and correctness, and *recombine them in new relations.* This last point is essential to successful mathematical study. The ideal must be cultivated if the mathematics are mastered.

5. Synthetic reflection promotes *generalization,*

Analytic reflection promotes *reasoning*. Comparison, united with ideality and a strict regard for the truth, promotes correct *judgment*. The power of correct generalization, reasoning, and judgment call into exercise the highest powers of the human mind. These powers are possessed, in any degree of perfection, only by the wisest of the human race. Teachers ought not to feel discouraged if young men and women under their care are slow in maturing these faculties. In many cases they do not reach any great degree of perfection. until middle life.

HOW TO PROMOTE HEALTHY CHILD-GROWTH.

Enough has been said to show that each child must have special study. The method of grading in some places is often more in accordance with age and size than personal endowments. Pupils of a certain age are put. into certain classes, whether they are fitted to be there or not, and kept there until they can pass the examinations. This is not according to the teaching of psychology. We must recognize in each child its own individuality.

1. The first thing, then, to do is to study the needs of each individual child, and afterward classify the school in accordance with the decisions arrived at. Some children need a great deal of out-door exercise. Let them have it. Nature is the best teacher. If we follow the indications of Nature we shall not go very far out of the way. It would be cruel to require a demure, sad, delicate child, who is naturally reflective and fond of reading and writing, to remain in a warm room, and push her on in her studies so that she may shine in the school as a brilliant scholar. Before she is a young woman she may injure her health if not hopelessly, yet in after-life she may become a ner-

vous wreck. The brilliant morning may close in a cloudy afternoon. On the other hand, the active, healthy, vigorous child, who is running and romping with all his might out-of-doors, and whose whole life is bound up in fun and frolic, will bear as much in-door work as it is possible to give him. There must be great flexibility if we expect our children to become strong and healthy in after-life.

2. The development of the mind of the child must be determined. In some, the reflective faculties develop quite early; in others, quite late. Some are very imaginative, and love poetry; others are not at all imaginative, and cannot bear to read poetry. Some children develop a mathematical faculty, and delight in arithmetic, and can very soon study the elements of geometry and algebra. Others are almost dunces in mathematics. In older times it was supposed that a child should be made to study that which he most disliked, in order to promote his equable development. For example, if his memory was poor, his memory should be trained directly. This is wrong. The training of the mind must proceed along the lines of the greatest activities, not along the lines of the least activities. Let us see what this means. If a child delights to read and write, but has a poor technical memory, let that child read and write to her heart's content. Let *the memory alone,* but give exercises in reproducing what is read or written, also in comparison and association. The

memory will be thus trained without giving words and dates to be committed to memory. Much is said now concerning the training of the retentive faculty, and the best conclusion of those who have studied the matter is that memory is strong in proportion as the observation, association, and imagination are strong. Careful habits of observation and the forming of habits of associating similar things will always strengthen the memory. In no other way can this work be accomplished.

Then wisdom shows us that we should give such children as have poor memories a great deal of observation work and association work, and it will be seen very soon that the memory will assert its power. For example, if a child dislikes to memorize dates in history, at first, *give no dates in history for the child to remember*. But what shall we do ? Take this course : Tell a story to-day, to-morrow tell another one; let it follow in the order of time after the preceding one; the next day tell another one—let this follow in the order of time. Now after several stories are told and reproduced, ask which one came first, which second, which third. Now, what relation has the second to the third, and so on. After the order of relationship has been established, then the date can come in; but not until this order of relationship has been established should the date be given. If this course be pursued, children will have no difficulty in remembering dates and names also. The reason that some children do not like number is because the faculty of *relation* is not developed; the child puzzles over his examples in arithmetic because he does not see the *relation* between their parts.   He reads, " A man bought a piece of ground for $500, and sold half of it for $300, and one fourth of the remainder for $200.   What did he make by the transaction ?"   Many children are entirely unable to solve such an example as this—not because it is difficult, but because the relations between the parts are not clearly seen.   Do not urge children on in mathematics faster than they can understand; but *urge them on* AS FAST AS POSSIBLE *in the direction they like to go,* and every month reclassify the school in reference to attainments. Very much more could be said under this head, but enough has been written to show in what directions children should receive impulses, and in what directions they should not.

3. Again, *healthy growth is natural growth,* and in accordance with natural activities. *Do not force in unnatural directions.*   Gnarly, misshapen, ugly results will be sure to appear.   Watch the trees, watch the growing plants in the spring; study the farmer as he cultivates his corn and potatoes, and imagine that the vegetables are children, and as nearly as possible imitate Nature. Follow Nature, and you will not be very far out of the way.

CONCERNING TEMPERAMENTAL DIFFERENCES.

Much can be said concerning this subject, but we have only space to condense a few thoughts that thinking teachers can easily make use of. Much that is said here can also be found in "Mind Studies for Young Teachers."

1. Determine the temperaments of your pupils. This means their physical characteristics and mental peculiarities.

2. Give more exercise and stimulus to the lymphatic and logy ones than to the nervous.

3. Do not put two pupils of the same temperament in the same seat.

4. Speak quietly and gently to the nervous child, and by no means point out publicly her mistakes. The lymphatic boy or girl needs a little more vigorous treatment. It should be kind, but it can be energetic.

5. Remember that nervous children do many things from impulse. This should be remembered in dealing with them. If a nervous child becomes angry and stubborn, let her alone. She will come to her senses, and a quiet, kind remark will bring everything around in a short time.

6. The nervous child needs direction. Many young teachers are very much afraid of saying no. It depends altogether in what spirit this littel word is uttered. It may be spoken in such a way as to rouse all the malignant passions of the soul, or it may be uttered in such a manner as to arouse the tenderest sympathies. Nervous children need government; but be careful that this government is full of kindness and love, and yet full of inflexibility, quiet determination, and courage.

7. A nervous-sanguine child will bear a great deal of firm government. Don't be afraid to say quietly, but firmly and kindly, "No." Tears will flow; angry, hasty words very likely be uttered; but don't mind: keep cool, collected, and firm; say little, and that little kindly, in a quieting tone of voice. The shower will pass, and with the tear-drop on the cheek the penitent regret will follow.

8. If the bilious temperament is mixed with a little lymphatic and a little nervous, there will often be difficulty of a serious nature. Outbursts of passion will not pleasantly pass away, but there will be sulkiness, moroseness, backbiting, and a disposition to stir up mischief. This needs careful treatment. The best way to treat such cases as this is: (1) ask the doing of a favor; (2) show confidence by assigning some special work where it is possible; (3) talk alone, and in a natural but decided tone of voice awaken the conscience; (4) be unyielding in action, but use great care how you

threaten or promise, or seem anxious to obtain personal favor; (5) if you have been wrong, say so in a manly manner, but not in a craven spirit; (6) keep the reins as in driving horses—in your own hands; (7) ask a skilful horse-trainer how he deals with a balky horse, and apply his wisdom to the child.

9. Because a lymphatic child is apparently stubborn, be careful that you do not mistake his motive. A nervous teacher trying to move a lymphatic boy to action by more nervousness is a ridiculous sight. The immobility of the one is only matched by the impatience of the other.

10. The temperaments most injured by injudicious teachers are the bilious and nervous. The sanguine and lymphatic will stand uninjured a great amount of abuse.

Many a bilious boy has been sent to the State's prison, if not to the gallows, by ignorant teachers.

General Notes.—1. Be certain you understand your child before you punish.

2. Be also certain the child understands you before you blame him.

3. General complaining remarks before the school are always out of place. No two pupils hear them alike.

4. The child of slow comprehension, sluggish movements, may in the long-run come out ahead.

5. The least hopeful temperament is the pure

bilious-lymphatic, when it has been subjected to wrong influences at home or in the street.

6. The most hopeful temperament is the nervous-lymphatic, when it has been properly trained at home or by associates.   .

7. Only by degrees can permanent changes be effected in temperament. *Be patient, but eternally persistent.*

WHAT WILL INSURE
A TEACHER'S SUCCESS,

AND BRING

Good Pay and a Permanent Place.

Motive is the power that drives life's work. Unless the motive is strong the motion will be slight. The teacher who does not expect to continue the work of instruction for any length of time has not sufficient motive to lead her to become thoroughly prepared in all branches of what she has undertaken. She is continually saying, "I may not teach another year," or "I may: it depends upon circumstances ; at least I am certain that I shall not continue in the work for many years; and why should I trouble myself about better preparation, since the effort I put forth will bring me neither more money nor greater popularity?" But the teacher who has risked everything is like the man who has expended all his money in buying a ship and freighting it with a cargo to a foreign land. He *must* succeed. If he does not he is ruined. The risk he has taken is too great to permit any carelessness. He employs the best help, he devotes himself with the greatest degree

---

Note.—The pages which follow on this subject are intended for those who are expecting to become life long teachers.

of earnestness towards making his voyage profitable. The probability is that such a man will succeed. Whole-heartedness is essential to success, but the teacher cannot be whole-hearted who has undertaken the work of teaching school as a stepping stone to something else. The young man who is expecting to become a minister, and teaches school to get money to help him prepare for his chosen profession, never attains any great degree of true success. His mind is beyond, not here. His reading is in the line of his life-work, not that of his temporary occupation. Now we come to our *first* head.

Those who become successful in teaching have an uquenchable desire to become successful.—This thought fills their minds day and night. They are continually asking for the means of attaining the highest success. Whenever a new book is opened they think, "Can I find anything here that will assist me?" Every educational paper is read with this thought uppermost in the mind. The biographies of successful men have to them this object distinctly in view. Sermons are turned to good account. Every public address for the year is used as a sponge from which to squeeze something nourishing to them. No one who has not this desire *constantly* in the mind will attain success.

A determination to use all possible efforts to become successful, is a second point. A great many people have desires, but they are too indolent to put forth the effort to attain their desires.

Thousands of men die poor, who had an earnest desire all their lives to become rich, but never had energy enough to make more than barely enough to supply the necessaries of life. No rich man ever held out his hands and received money from the heavens. He planned and worked with a downright earnest effort and persistent determination to reach the object of his desires. Napoleon was not a very good man, but he was a very determined one, and he had a mighty intellect to guide him in attaining the object of his choice. General Grant's will is known, and his maxim, "I will fight it out on this line if it takes all summer," indicates his inflexible determination, or as the papers call it "doggedness" of his mind. The teacher who adds to a sincere desire to become successful, the determination that leads her to say, *"I will become successful,"* will put forth all possible efforts to attain her object, and it needs no prophet, or the son of a prophet, to predict that such an one will reach the end of her ambition.

All of this is but preliminary to the object for which this article was prepared. The subject of the greatest importance to be considered by all teachers is :—

What will make my teaching a success? *Knowing what true success is.* The savage is frequently successful up to the light he has, but his standard is very low, yet it is all the standard he knows anything about. Our ideals rule our characters. *A person having no knowledge of what a*

*good school is cannot by any means teach a good
school*, even though he might be ever so successful
and diligent. For example, some teachers think
that the highest success in teaching consists in
keeping the pupils quiet. They are frequently repeating the common maxim, " Order is heaven's
first law," but they have no true idea of what order
is. They require their pupils to sit still with
folded hands and fixed gaze, whenever they are not
studying their lessons. Military precision is to
them the perfection of order, whereas it may be,
and frequently is, the very perfection of disorder.

*The true ideal of what successful teaching is
can only be obtained by knowing something about
the capacity of the child*, his heavenly origin and
his immortal destiny. The teacher who treats a
child as a receptacle to be filled with a certain
amount of knowledge has no more idea of the destiny of a human being than he whose business it is
to fill quart bowls or forty-gallon barrels. The immortal Pestalozzi said that " The number of facts
a pupil learns is by no means the measure of his
success." Like all other general statements, this is
both true and false, for the number of facts a pupil *learns* by his own efforts, has a great deal to do
with the measure of his success. On the other
hand, the number of words a pupil commits to
memory, without understanding what those words
mean, is not only no measure of the pupil's success,
but an obstacle standing in the way of his success.
A teacher ignorant of what teaching is requires

her pupils to commit to memory the dates of history. They become very successful doing this work, but they have no knowledge of the relation of facts connected with these dates, only they know when certain events occurred, and on examination they are able to give a great number of them correctly. The people applaud the child, and the teacher receives great praise. But she does not deserve it. On the other hand, she deserves great condemnation. She has done an irreparable injury to her pupils, for every sentence committed to memory without thoroughly understanding what the words mean will remain as an obstacle in the mind of the child during all of its life, hindering both the reception of knowledge and its useful application. Too much cannot be said on this subject.

In order to become a good teacher good books on teaching must be read. Especially we commend for careful study Page's "Theory and Practice of Teaching," and Fitch's "Lectures on Teaching." Another excellent book, perhaps equal to these two and in some respects superior, is Payne's "Lectures on the Science and Art of Education." Read these books carefully, and they will be of immense benefit. Another book that treats of character in general more than teaching in particular, is "Self-culture," by James Freeman Clarke. Some of the chapters in this work have never been equalled by any author in the English language. If one book only can be obtained this would be the one, not only to read, but to study and apply.

Again, success demands powers of quick and accurate observation. A great many "see men as trees walking ;" it is not to be supposed that such persons will ever know very much, for they have never seen very much. It is astonishing how little the average person sees that he thinks he sees, or knows what he thinks he knows. How few can tell how many legs a spider or common house-fly has, or whether a cat has more toes on its front than its hind feet ; and yet these people have seen spiders, flies and cats all their lives. Ask the average woman why a fish dies when it is taken out of the water, or why a man dies when he is under the water, and she cannot'tell. These points show the want of quick and accurate observation on the part of those who have good eyes and good ears and no defect in their organs of speech. The habit of mispronunciation of words is unfortunate, and comes, frequently, from carelessness. How many people persist in articulating the t in *often*, when, if they noticed, they would see that no person who speaks the language correctly pronounces this word in that way. And what is true of this word is true of a thousand other words. All great inventors have become such through the powers of seeing and thinking. Howe made a fortune by simply putting the eye of a needle near its point. Why had not some one thought of doing that before and thus invented the sewing machine ? But nobody had, for nobody before Howe had ever thought it could be done, and yet when it was done, everybody said, "That's easy enough ! Why didn't I think of that !" Yes, "Why *didn't* they think of it?" Because they hadn't the mind. All of Edison's inventions have been made through the cultivation of his powers of seeing accurately and quickly and reasoning correctly. The stupid fool goes on straight to destruction, because he does not see that the road he is travelling in leads there ; the wise man just behind him looks up and sees plainly where the road is leading him, and he turns about and travels the other way—the foolish pass on and are punished. Pres. Hill, when a school committee man in Massachusetts, used to examine pupils by putting five or six beans in his hand, quickly opening it and asking them to tell him at once how many there were. At first they could not tell, but soon they could count at sight up to ten or twelve. A certain very successful man trained himself to habits of quick and accurate observation so thoroughly that, after standing before the large show window of a dry goods store for five minutes, he could go home and write an accurate description of everything that was displayed, and tell exactly their positions. He reached this excellence by gradual steps ; first by observing a few things and then a few more, and so on until his mind could grasp the almost numberless objects in the entire window. A teacher of quick observation will notice the begin-

ning of trouble long before the pupils see it.   It is
easy to stop the beginnings, but, oh, how hard it
is to stem the rushing tide at the end ! So we
say that powers of quick and accurate observation
are essential to teaching success.   We have not
space here to point out how these qualities may be
obtained : friends must be consulted, books must
be read in order to ascertain the means to reach
this important end.   But that *they must be had*
before there is any great degree of school-room
success must be obvious to any thinking mind.

**Again, there must be sympathy and heart kind-
ness.** This must be genuine ; deception in the
school-room is easily detected ; children see very
quickly through hypocrisy.   It is a flimsy garment
at best, and does not serve to cover up the hideous
nakedness of evil in its original form.   A teacher
who has not a good heart and genuine sympathy
for children would do well to stay out of the school-
room.   She may drive herself and her pupils
through a round of duties day after day and term
after term, but she will have trouble and difficulty and distress, and at last the consciousness
if not the public verdict of failure.   Many instances could be narrated of teachers who have
not done their pupils much good on account of
their want of sympathy.   The young heart of
childhood yearns for nothing so much as love ; it
is full of impulse and affection, and when it finds
affection in return, its sympathies go out in a full
end overflowing tide.   Of course there are occa-

sional exceptions, but the majority of children can easily be touched by a sympathetic look and the token of love. This is not gushing, for gushing is nothing but modified hypocrisy; it is genuine sympathy—affection of the best and truest kind.

A teacher who has no appreciation of the wants of childhood, its difficulties, trials, and discouragements, cannot do children *little* good. How often are children seen to cry for some minutes as though their hearts would break. Can we measure the woe and misery of that brief time? To an older person the disappointments of a child seem very trivial. Most are disposed to laugh at the woes of a little child crying for a worthless toy. But consider how we appear to beings superior to us when we lament over the loss of baubles which to them are more worthless than the toy was to that child. They know too much to laugh at us, but while they pity our stupidity, they have a deep sympathy for us; as should we have for the woes of our children.

And then, *the doing good because we like to do good,* is a noble incentive. How different this is from doing good because we *ought* to do good. There is a wide difference between *ought* and *like* in these relations. One person drags herself through a round of duties, reading the Bible against her will, praying contrary to her wishes and inclinations, and going to church from a sense of duty and not for the love of it. She makes a poor miserable Christian at the best, but when the heart is full of joy, when the page of the Bible is luminous with helpfulness and interest, and when all the means the church gives bring peace and comfort to the soul, then how beautiful are the gates of Zion and how happy are those who attend her joyous feasts! So with such buoyant heart and glad exaltation should the teacher enter the school! Then will the work be a true success, even though it may be marred by many scholastic failures, and pedagogical sins !

A very important element entering into teaching success is sound reason, good judgment and self-control. There are thousands of people who say, " if my foresight was as good as my hindsight, I should have made a great success in this world." What is the reason that the foresight is so poor? It is a want of reason. Impulse has ruled them. People act on the spur on the moment ; they decide without thinking, conclude without judging and let their impulses run away them. It does not need a prophet to predict that such people will always be in hot water. They have not minds of their own. Now there are frequent times when a wise deliberation is the quickest way to decide a difficult question. There was once a surgeon in the French army who was called to the side of an officer who had received a serious wound. An important artery was cut in two and his life blood was rapidly ebbing away. He waited for half a minute without doing anything. Those around him were violent in their denunciation of his dilatoriness,

A half minute is a long time when a man's life is trembling in the balance, and it seemed to the by-standers as though he had waited ten times as long as he did ; but at the end of the half minute he went right to work and before the second half minute had expired the blood was stopped, the operation had been successfully performed, and the man's life was saved. After he was through, they asked him "What made you wait so long before you commenced to work, doctor ? " His answer is worthy a permanent record, "I took time to be certain that what I did was the right thing to do. I knew the man had a minute to live, and I determined to take half that time in deciding what was the best course to take." Had he acted hastily the probability is that the officer would have died. Instances often occur in which deliberation is very necessary in order to save life. A child has fallen in the water and is on the point of drowning, or a child has been in the water so long that consciousness has departed, or a pupil is choking to death, or has cut an artery, or has fainted away, or is in a fit. Now calmness is necessary, self-possession is all-important, and a good judgment is needed in order that the right thing may be done. When a person is in danger of dying for want of immediate help it does no good to run around like a chicken with its head off. We have known some people who in a case of danger would sit down and cry, wringing their hands, and saying, "O dear ! O dear ! O dear !" Such people are of very little account when emergencies arise. Thousands of lives have been sacrificed, that could have been saved if a little calmness and judgment had been used. Nearly all the cases of difficulty in school government come from a want of deliberation. A teacher once waited a whole day before she said anything to a very wicked pupil concerning a flagrant breach of propriety. She took time to make up her mind what she ought to say and do, and then, when she acted, she was certain that she was doing and saying the right thing. So in instruction the way to decide what the best method of teaching is, is to take time to ascertain the facts in the case. Thousands of teachers simply follow their noses and do what others have done, without thinking and reasoning and judging. The result is they do wrong, get themselves in trouble, and are condemned by those who are good judges. And yet we have known teachers who would insist, in spite of the determination of those whose opinions ought to be respected, to go right on year after year doing as they have been accustomed to do before. It is a singular fact in human nature that people with little reason and poor judgment and poor self-control are generally very stubborn. This is a fact in human experience that can be verified by every one who will take the trouble to observe the various phases of human nature.

Now we come to more specific directions in reference to teaching success ; what has gone before has been general, now we come to special ways for

teachers who desire to become successful and receive good pay and permanent places.

First, there must be good ideals. We never rise
above our ideals. A savage is satisfied with his
tepe, a Hottentot with his hut, and a Chinaman
with his crowded and contracted house. In order
to note what good teaching and what a school is,
good schools must be visited and good teachers
must be known. It is worth all it costs to observe
good teaching and good schools for several weeks,
even though such observation would require a
journey across the State or even across a continent.
We learn by seeing and doing far more than by
reading and meditating. There must be in the
mind of the teacher an *intense dissatisfaction.*
This will lead to an effort towards better things.
The country teacher who is perfectly satisfied with
her barn of a school-house, its miserable surroundings, its unshaded and slovenly grounds, its incon-
venient and rickety desks and the dirt and squalor
of her children, will not attempt to get anything
better.

It seems very ungracious to urge teachers to become dissatisfied with themselves, but there is a
great deal of wisdom in this counsel. An intense
longing to do better is a mighty power contribut-
ing to better doing. The parents in most of our
small village and district schools have a very low
ideals concerning what good teaching is, and teachers in these places are very apt to be satisfied when
they please their patrons. Now it is safe to say

that those teachers who attempt no more than to please uneducated and ignorant fathers and mothers will never rise in the work of teaching. They will always receive poor salaries and never be certain of one place any great length of time. When any young man or young women is considered fit to teach school, all the young men and the young women in the surrounding country are continually crowding each other to the wall. But if the conviction is in the mind of the people that the teacher must be educated before she can teach school, then only educated teachers will be chosen for teaching positions.

Among the means of attaining success within the reach of those who cannot go through a thorough course of study and graduate at a first-class State Normal School are, Teachers' Associations, Teachers' Institutes, and Summer Schools.

1. Teachers' Associations. These are often very good. Sometimes they are not, but usually a teacher will gain much good by attending them. Contact with superior teachers is an excellent thing. The listening to discussions and the hearing of thoughtful papers are uplifting, but we should earnestly advise all those teachers who are anxious to attain success, to take *active* parts in these associations. Those who do not, but quietly listen and then go away without saying anything or doing anything, will ordinarily get little good. The effort required in the preparation of a paper to be read before an association of teachers is a mighty force. Suppose the subject assigned is "Best Methods of Teaching Geography." The one preparing the essay should buy all the books within her means on this subject, such as King's, Parker's, Frye's, Geikie's and others. She should read these books with great care, then she should visit the best school within her reach, and notice the methods used there. If she wished to go still deeper in the subject, she would read Guyot's "Earth and Man," and Ritter's "Geographical Studies." She should also become thoroughly familiar with the methods of teaching *both* physical and political, astronomical and mathematical geography. Now it is safe to say that after one had thus prepared herself for six months, she would present before an association a paper of great value. The difficulty with teachers' associations frequently is that there is not sufficient effort put forth in the preparation of the articles; but valuable papers, such as we have described, are becoming more and more common, and more and more are teachers' associations becoming helpful to those who have an earnest desire to be helped.

2. **Teachers' Institutes.** These are now common in all the counties of our country, and many of them are excellent, although some are very poor. The State of New York, for example, employs a number of experienced teachers to go from county to county and instruct the teachers in the best methods of teaching. Of course some things are said and done that are not very uplifting, but with

few exceptions the teacher that attends a county institute for a week with a sincere desire to get good will not fail to receive great good. Teachers' institutes are short normal schools where classes are often taught in the presence of the teachers. Do not be afraid at an institute to asks questions. Seek the acquaintance of the conductors for the purpose of receiving from them all the good you can. Friendships are formed at associations and institutes that are frequently of great use in securing better places. If a teacher is really doing good work the world should know it. It is only by becoming acquainted with those who have wide knowledge of men and things that a good teacher is discovered and taken out from her humble surroundings and given larger pay and a more permanent place. Institute conductors are always on the lookout for the best teachers. No persons are more frequently consulted than they in reference to the qualifications of their pupils. So in many ways the County Institute can be made a powerful means for promoting teaching success. Those who use it for the purpose of social advantages, or as a week of recreation, lose a great deal of good that otherwise might be obtained.

Third, Summer Schools. These are of recent origin, but evidently have become a permanent part of our educational work. In these schools the teacher can mingle pleasure with profit. There are no more delightful places in the country than Asbury Park, Saratoga Springs, Martha's

Vineyard, Glens Falls, Lake Minnetonka, Minn. and Madison, Wis. At all these places summer schools are established, and the cost of tuition and board is reduced to the lowest possible amount. These schools are more profitable than teachers' institutes, for they continue longer, and thus give an opportunity for the members to systematize and extend their work more thoroughly. We would earnestly advise all teachers who are aiming at success and who cannot stop the work of teaching to attend a normal school, to make arrangements to attend a summer school. In some respects, we believe, they are the best normal schools in the country. Earnest teachers are met there who have devoted their lives to teaching and are eager for information and improvement. The teachers of these schools are selected with great care, and almost without exception are men and women of superior abilities. Here the opportunity is given to become more thoroughly prepared in the subject matter of the branches taught, especially at Martha's Vineyard in the various departments of natural science.

The Power of a Living Teacher. In studying any subject, as botany, zoology, chemistry or physics, a teacher is a great help; no book can take the place of a living instructor. The analyzing of a plant with a capable botanist gives more of education and help than the solitary study of botany for a long time ; in fact nothing can be placed before the inspiration and helpfulness of contact with a successful teacher, both in learning the natural sciences and the modern languages. Probably the best summer school for the study of the languages is at Amherst College, Mass.

Before visiting other schools, attending an institute or becoming a member of a summer school, one thing is very necessary. This is *a knowledge of what is desired to be learned.* Many teachers go to institutes and summer schools and fail of getting any benefit from them because they attempt to do too much. They think, " I have but little time and little money, and I must get everything I can—nothing must be omitted." So they attend every class, hear every lecture, get up early in the morning, sit up late at night, and in the end are wearied, tired, confused and discouraged. True improvement is a plant of slow growth. No one on the spur of the moment can become very much better than he is, but he can gradually improve, and so in the course of a year or two make substantial progress. But personal improvement leading to success must be attained by *judicious work of the proper kind, at the proper times.* This is very important counsel, which those who are aiming at success would do well to read over several times.

In order to find out what you need, learn all that you can before you attend an institute or a summer school. This can be done by reading the right kind of educational literature. A few books are extremely important, and should be thoroughly studied. Next to Page's "Theory and Practice of Teaching" there is not a better book in the English language than Parker's "Talks on Teaching." Following this, read Fitch's "Art of Questioning," "Art of Securing and Retaining Attention," and "Improvement in the Art of. Teaching," "Kellogg's "School Management," Calkins' "Eye and Voice Training," Dewey's "How to teach Manners in the School-room," Seeley's Grube's "Method in Teaching Arithmetic," and Woodhull's "Simple Experiments for the School-room." These books will give to the inquiring teacher a large number of most valuable suggestions which will be a great help in attaining true success. They should be studied, not skimmed over,—read carefully, and not hurriedly glanced at. Those who attend institutes and summer schools will find many of the suggestions given by instructors in these schools modifications of those found in these books; whatever of good in addition is obtained will be so much gain, and thus so much more valuable stock in trade.

1. Apparatus. Why should not a teacher have a good "kit" as well as the brick-layer or carpenter? Whenever a master builder attempts to construct a house, he brings with him not only his workmen but his tools. Why should not a teacher as well have a quantity of "tools" with which to work? These would be of inestimable value. After a few years they would increase at very slight expense, and yet in the aggregate, become extremely valuable. For example, a little skill will enable almost any teacher to make raised maps of each of the five continents in plaster of Paris, coloring them properly and mounting them in such a manner as to be the least liable to harm from usage. These in the school-room could be models from which the pupils could construct others in putty or sand. Again, with a little expense large pictures of notable persons could be cut from the illustrated newspapers, also illustrations of events and scenes in various parts of the world. These could be pasted on a chart, neatly bound and hung, when needed, in the school-room. Do not keep these charts in the presence of the pupils all the time; they will lose their interest in them if you do. Use them only when needed— and the day before state that to-morrow you will show them such and such pictures or things. The interest of the pupils will be excited, their expectation will be aroused into healthy activity. All of these excitements to the mind will assist in fixing what may be said. We have known many teachers who have collected a large number of illustrations which have been of very great use in language work, as well as illustrations of general talks before the school, and we know that these teachers have attained a very much greater degree of success by the use of such aids than they possibly could without them. The extent to which charts of this nature could be provided is only limited by the number of illustrated papers the teacher is able to buy.

2. There are many kindergarten helps that can be made of great use in primary and intermediate departments : Blocks, sticks, different colored worsteds, bits of colored paper, several pairs of scissors, a small portable table. For about fifteen dollars a teacher could provide herself with all of the esentials of the kindergarten apparatus, and most of it could be made use of in the higher departments.

Again: **3. Collections can be made of interesting objects about which talks could be given.** Different kinds of seeds, nuts, grains, materials for food, woods, foreign drugs, both liquid and solid, and simple minerals as well as rocks and common stones. These should be placed in small boxes, carefully labelled and arranged so that they can be obtained at a moment's notice. Every collection is worthless unless the collector knows at once where to find each individual specimen. In the one department of seeds there is an opportunity of arranging a very large number; then there could also be among them dried specimens of insects and preserved animals in small bottles of liquor. The extent to which this work could be carried is practically unlimited. We know that the ordinary teacher would not be able to spend a very large sum each year, but a great deal of money is not needed. Very valuable specimens of various kinds can be obtained in almost every school district in this land. Those living on the sea shore could arrange to exchange specimens with teachers living in the mountainous districts, and thus each part of the country be provided with that which would be especially interesting, strange and useful.

Again: **4. By a little skill and effort very valuable maps can be made and mounted;** in fact, maps more valuable than could be purchased. If teachers would make but one such map each term, in the course of a few years the collection would be of great use. Especially should the teacher make a careful and correct map of the district in which she teaches. This should be on a large scale, and pupils should be instructed to copy it and talk about it, pointing out the objects found in its various parts. This will do almost more than anything else to get into the minds of pupils the true geographical conception of the world, an idea which comparatively few pupils, after the old method of teaching geography, ever receive. If we cannot see in the mind's eye that which we are accustomed to see with the external eye, how can we see in the mind's eye that which we cannot see with the external eye? Unless the pupils in geography have a vivid conception in the mind of the appearance of the country *as it really is*, they are not studying geography, but words, facts, dates. The drawing of a map be the most senseless work a pupil can do, or it may be the very best work that he does. It depends upon whether the map gives to his mind a clear, distinct view of the part of the world represented.

5. Again, other aids the teacher can make great use of in the school-room are EDUCATIONAL PAPERS. By all means take a weekly journal ; it is too long to wait a whole month for an educational paper to come, and when it does come, it does not contain enough to satisfy the educational hunger of the teacher who is anxious for success. The teacher who cannot afford $2.50 for a first-rate weekly educational journal like the SCHOOL JOURNAL, cannot afford to buy a new pair of shoes once a year.

The weekly paper comes freighted with the most valuable material for the working teacher ; it may be perhaps but a single article, or, occasionally, there may be a single paragraph, and yet that article, or that paragraph, will help more than the money paid for the whole year's subscription. There are some teachers whose pay is small, and who do not expect to continue in the work of teaching but a short time, who will find a monthly paper valuable. To such we would commend the TEACHERS' INSTITUTE. It is full of hints that cannot fail to be of great assistance to teachers who have had but limited experience and opportunities.

Other apparatus, like globes, electrical machines, air pumps, barometers, thermometers, etc., etc., can be obtained if the teacher's purse is long enough. The average school director is so little interested in a knowledge of school needs that he will not be apt to buy necessary aids ; and the time has not come, in most district schools, for the people to anticipate the wants of teachers ; but we believe the time has come when it will pay for the teacher to use all energy within her power, and, for a few years, all the money she can spare, to provide herself with all the necessary appliances for her work.

6. Another means of attaining success is *general information*. By this is meant a knowledge of persons, places, and things. Suppose something has been said in the school-room about Rome. It gives pupils a great deal of confidence to find that the teacher knows something about the "Eternal City,"—perhaps some incident or some fact connected with its early history. A teacher should be thoroughly familiar with the political and religious questions of the day. The time has gone by in enlightened places when any one is persecuted for opinion's sake, and it is very well that it has. Every individual is allowed to express his belief on all subjects at proper times without danger from the state. It has been but a short time since this order of things commenced, for in older times it was considered a most improper thing for any person to form his own opinion. *A teacher who has pronounced convictions on the great political questions of the day, and on all proper occasions expresses them, will make a far better teacher than one who is ignorant of these subjects.* Supposing that during an evening's conversation something should be said concerning Abraham Lincoln. How much it would add to the interest of the occasion or gathering to hear a good story told about Lincoln's early life or mature years. How much does it add confidence in the laborer to hear his employer give his commands in an intelligent manner. The one who has no opinion on politics or religion, or the one who has opinions, but is not willing to express them for fear of making somebody angry, will always fill a very subordinate place in the work of the world. It cannot be otherwise. The teacher who has general information is always ready, on a moment's notice, to say something to his pupils both interesting and profitable. All must concede this to be very important. How it adds to the interest of the history class for the teacher to narrate a story concerning some one about whom they have been studying. Like begets like. A dull teacher who plods on in the footsteps of his predecessors has little influence for good.

In the foregoing pages much has been said of special value to the teacher *as a teacher ;* now we wish to say a few words, in conclusion, concerning the elements of success in the teacher *as a citizen and member of society.*

1. Social. It is said that a teacher should never forget that she is a teacher, even in the family or social gathering. This is wrong advice. The native dignity and good sense of any one who has had charge of a school-room will indicate that pro-

priety and decorum should always be observed. In
visiting parents, be careful about assuming a dicta-
torial manner ; also, be careful about appearing to
patronize parents. There was once a good minister,
who said he always ingratiated himself into the
affections of a mother by trotting the baby on his
knee. It must be admitted that there are certain
times when this would be proper ; but there are
other times when this would be obviously improper.
In visiting a family where there has been trouble
with some member of it in the school, it is best to
talk as little as possible about the difficulty, and as
much as possible about other and more cheerful
subjects. There was once a bad boy who was
upheld in his waywardness by his parents, and the
teacher determined that she would visit the family,
and talk with them about their son. But an after-
thought determined her to change her mind. She
visited the family, and took tea with them, and
talked very pleasantly about a dozen things ; but
never said a word about their son. When she was
gone, the father turned to the boy, and said :
" John, she is a good woman ; I like her first-rate,
and you must do nothing to annoy her. You have
been a bad boy ; now be a good boy." When the
boy found that he was not upheld by the parents,
but that they had confidence in the teacher, he
soon stopped his pranks, and became a good
scholar. Now, if this teacher had disgraced the
boy, she would soon have found herself in trouble.
She pursued the wisest course, and teachers can

learn lessons from her example. Talk always fans the flame, and adds fuel to personal controversy. Most people talk too much, and teachers in a school frequently get themselves into great trouble by too free use of their tongues.

In social gatherings, where parents and pupils mingle on an equality with the teacher, much can be done to strengthen the regard in which the teacher is held, by interesting exercises, games, plays, etc., that will be both attractive and beneficial. While the teacher should not waste her time in attending social gatherings, yet if she refuses to mingle with the people, she will lose a great deal of her influence over them. There are many objectionable games in some parts of our country that would soon be withdrawn if some sensible ones were introduced in their place. It is the want of knowledge that causes people to waste their time in frivolity, rather than the presence of depravity. In most schools of the country, the religious element is very strong, and the teacher will gain a great deal of power and influence by attending the church and taking part in the Sabbath-school. Distinctive religious instruction is forbidden in the public schools in this country, ubt it is not forbidden in the church and Sabbath-school. Here the teacher can make herself felt as nowhere else. Hence, she can easily be a leader, and the foremost promoter of every good cause.

2. A teacher's success is also very much promoted *by introducing good reading in the families of the* *district.* Papers of a low character get into a village because the people do not know the value of papers of a different sort. Some of the most interesting books at the present time are of a very high character. The tone of interesting stories has been growing better and better for the last ten years. There is no lack of excellent papers, which children will delight to read if they once get hold of them. Every district ought to have a circulating library, composed of the best books. Since stories are read more generally than any other class of literature, the best stories could be selected, one book serving for the whole neighborhood. The cost of a library, right up to the times, would be but little, and its value would be very great. Do not expect the children or the people to read a book because it is good. There is nothing in this world like interest. A volume of prosy old sermons would not bring much at a public auction ; but a volume of live, bright stories, discussing the things of to-day, would bring their full market value. The world is full of interesting books ; and when the people once get a taste of them, they will have as many of them as they can buy.

3. Again, an element in the teacher's success is *want of success.* If you have failed, consider it your gain. You will only learn by experience ; but do not repeat the same mistake twice. If a failure has taught you a lesson, it is worth all that it costs. Some people go on year after year repeating the mistakes of the past. Such never improve ; but wise men learn by their mistakes, and thus, as they grow older, grow wiser and more successful.

4. Work just as hard whether your pay is good or poor. Do not gauge the quality of your work, or the amount of your work, by the pay you receive. This is good advice—perhaps the best given on these pages. If you have undertaken to do a piece of work, do it to the very best of your ability, and not slight it because the amount of money you are to receive for it is less than you think you ought to get.

5. Now, in the end, *save some money ;* if your salary is small, you can save a little ; but if it is good you should save considerable. It is an element of success for a teacher to feel that she has a little money on hand for a "rainy day," and that when her work ceases she will not be cast upon the charities of the world. A little saved, and well invested, often produces a great deal ; and then the habit of saving is one that will produce an excellent effect upon the mind and heart. A certain degree of independence is needed, in order to properly succeed ; and the feeling constantly in the mind, that we have no money at all, is apt to produce depression and a feeling of dependence which is not conducive to a great degree of success. Therefore, we say, save a little money each week, or each year, and you will find it the best investment you ever made, whether you consider it in the light of its pecuniary advantage or its mental,

moral, and physical influence. Last, LOVE GOD
AND KEEP HIS COMMANDMENTS. Be cheerful,
take care of your health, but by all means guard
your *conscience*. Read the best books and the best
papers, associate with the best people, and do not
be discouraged at failures.